WOMEN
GROUNDBREAKERS

WOMEN IN POLITICS

Miriam Coleman

PowerKiDS press™

New York

D1318496

Published in 2016 by The Rosen Publishing Group, Inc.
29 East 21st Street, New York, NY 10010

First Edition

Editor: Sarah Machajewski
Book Design: Reann Nye

Photo Credits: Cover (background) Gts/Shutterstock.com; cover (Rice) STAN HONDA/AFP/Getty Images; cover (Clinton) ERIC FEFERBERG/AFP/Getty Images; cover (Sotomayor) http://commons.wikimedia. org/wiki/File:Sonia_Sotomayor_in_SCOTUS_robe.jpg; p. 5 http://commons.wikimedia.org/wiki/ File:Susan_B_Anthony_c1855.png; p. 7 FPG/Archive Photos/Getty Images; p. 9 Hulton Archive/Hulton Archive/Getty Images; p. 10 Fox Photos/Hulton Archive/Getty Images; p. 11 Fotosearch/Archive Photos/ Getty Images; p. 13 New York Daily News Archive/New York Daily News/Getty Images; p. 14 Neftali/ Shutterstock.com; p. 15 Dirck Halstead/The LIFE Images Collection/Getty Images; p. 17 Rogers/Hulton Archive/Getty Images; p. 19 (O'Connor) Keystone/Hulton Archive/Getty Images; p. 19 (Sotomayor) Win McNamee/Getty Images News/Getty Images; p. 21 PAUL J. RICHARDS/AFP/Getty Images; p. 23 Chris Hondros/Hulton Archive/Getty Images; p. 25 Terry Ashe/The LIFE Images Collection/ Getty Images; p. 27 Mike Coppola/Getty Images Entertainment/Getty Images; p. 29 Bloomberg/ Bloomberg/Getty Images.

Library of Congress Cataloging-in-Publication Data

Coleman, Miriam.
  Women in politics / Miriam Coleman.
      pages cm. — (Women groundbreakers)
  Includes bibliographical references and index.
  ISBN 978-1-4994-1046-4 (pbk.)
  ISBN 978-1-4994-1075-4 (6 pack)
  ISBN 978-1-4994-1084-6 (library binding)
  1. Women—Political activity—Juvenile literature. 2. Women public officers—Juvenile literature. 3. Women politicians—Juvenile literature. I. Title.
  HQ1236.C563 2016
  320.082—dc23
                              2015006139

Manufactured in the United States of America

CPSIA Compliance Information: Batch #WS15PK: For Further Information contact Rosen Publishing, New York, New York at 1-800-237-9932

CONTENTS

FIGHTING FOR A VOICE

In 1872, Susan B. Anthony was arrested in Rochester, New York, along with several other women. Her crime was casting a vote in the presidential election when women hadn't yet been granted the right to vote. She was punished with a fine of $100. Anthony refused to pay the fine and used her case to rally more Americans to the cause of women's **suffrage**.

Hundreds more women were arrested while fighting for a voice in American politics before women finally won the right to vote in 1920, when the Nineteenth Amendment to the Constitution passed. Today, almost a century later, women participate in politics on every level, thanks to the hard-fighting spirit of women like Anthony and her fellow suffragists.

Susan B. Anthony was instrumental in gaining equal political rights for women.

A SUFFRAGIST IN CONGRESS

Jeannette Rankin was the first woman to serve in the U.S. House of Representatives. Remarkably, she was elected to Congress at a time when women in many states didn't yet have the right to vote.

Rankin worked as a teacher, seamstress, and social worker before running to represent Montana in Congress in 1916. Once in office, she helped pass the Nineteenth Amendment and fought for the rights of women workers. Rankin was also a **pacifist** and voted against the United States entering World War I.

After finishing her term in 1919, Rankin continued working for pacifist causes and served as a delegate to the Women's International Conference for Peace in Switzerland. She was elected to Congress a second time in 1939.

AMAZING ACHIEVEMENTS

Rankin helped create Congress's Committee on Woman Suffrage in 1917. She joined the committee once it was created.

After being elected in 1916, Rankin said, "I may be the first woman member of Congress, but I won't be the last."

FIRST LADY OF THE WORLD

Until Eleanor Roosevelt came to the White House, First Ladies were expected to keep their opinions to themselves. However, Roosevelt wasn't afraid to speak her mind. She acted behind the scenes as a valuable political advisor to her husband, President Franklin Delano Roosevelt (FDR), and was the first First Lady to hold her own press conferences. She even wrote a daily newspaper column called "My Day."

Roosevelt had always been eager to help the **disadvantaged**. As a young woman, she volunteered to teach poor **immigrant** families in New York City. During World War I, she worked with the American Red Cross and volunteered at navy hospitals. When her husband was **paralyzed** by polio in 1921, she became increasingly active in politics, saying she was acting as the president's "eyes, ears, and legs."

AMAZING ACHIEVEMENTS

Because FDR was in office as president for four terms, Eleanor Roosevelt is the nation's longest-serving First Lady.

Roosevelt was active in the American Red Cross. She's pictured here addressing the public to ask for contributions to the organization.

FDR became president in 1933. He took office in the midst of the Great Depression—a time of terrible poverty and suffering across the nation. As First Lady, Eleanor Roosevelt worked to make sure her husband's policies helped Americans in need. She also championed **civil rights** for African Americans and traveled the country giving speeches to rally Americans to support the causes she believed in.

After FDR's death in 1945, Roosevelt remained active in politics. She was appointed U.S. delegate to the United Nations (UN) in 1946 and served as head of the UN Human Rights Commission. She became known as the "First Lady of the world." She continued fighting for better opportunities for women and civil rights for everyone until the end of her life in 1962.

Eleanor Roosevelt led the United Nations committee that wrote the Universal Declaration of Human Rights. This document states the rights and freedoms all people in the world are entitled to. Here, Roosevelt is pictured holding the historic document she helped create.

"UNBOUGHT AND UNBOSSED"

Shirley Chisholm was a true pioneer. Drawing on her background as an educator and **activist** in Brooklyn, New York, Chisholm became the first African American congresswoman and the first woman to seek the Democratic presidential nomination.

Chisholm was first elected to Congress as a Democrat from New York in 1968 and went on to serve seven terms. Declaring she had "no intention of just sitting quietly and observing," she helped found the Congressional Black **Caucus** and the National Women's Political Caucus while fighting hard for the rights of women, **minorities**, and the poor. While in office, she helped expand the nation's food stamp program to help feed low-income families. She also spoke out strongly against the Vietnam War.

AMAZING ACHIEVEMENTS

Chisholm held a bachelor's degree from Brooklyn College and a master's degree from Columbia University.

Chisholm once said, "I have a way of talking that does something to people…you have to let them feel you."

Chisholm's **slogan** for her first congressional campaign was "Unbought and Unbossed," which showed her dislike of dishonesty in the political system. She used the slogan again in 1972 when she ran for the Democratic nomination for president, saying she was the only candidate who stood for the interests of African Americans and poor people in inner cities. In the Democratic **primary**, Chisholm lost the election with just 10 percent of the vote. Though she lost, she made a strong impression on the nation.

Chisholm left Congress in 1983. She went on to teach politics and women's studies at Mount Holyoke College in Massachusetts and cofounded the National Political Congress of Black Women.

BLACK HERITAGE

USA FOREVER

SHIRLEY CHISHOLM

AMAZING ACHIEVEMENTS

The United States Postal Service honored Chisholm with a postage stamp in 2013.

Chisholm was elected to the National Women's Hall of Fame in 1993. She died in 2005.

THE IRON LADY

Margaret Thatcher was Great Britain's first female prime minister. Nicknamed the "Iron Lady," Thatcher was known for her position against the **Soviet Union** as well as the difficult and sometimes unpopular solutions she found to help Britain's economy.

As leader of the Conservative Party, Thatcher became prime minister when her party won the election in 1979. It was a time of great economic trouble for Britain, and many people were out of work. Thatcher worked with her government to fix these problems. The policies she set changed the country for years to come. With three election victories in a row, she ended up holding office for 11 years—longer than any other British politician in the 20th century.

AMAZING ACHIEVEMENTS

Thatcher studied chemistry at Oxford University, but wanted to get into politics. She first ran to become a member of Parliament, the United Kingdom's lawmaking body, when she was 23. She was finally elected in 1959, when she was 34.

Ronald Reagan

Margaret Thatcher

Thatcher helped mend the tense **relationship** between the United States and the Soviet Union during the 1980s. Here, she's pictured with U.S. president Ronald Reagan.

THE NATION'S HIGHEST COURT

After earning a law degree in 1952, Sandra Day O'Connor set out to find a job, but discovered no firm was willing to hire a woman as a lawyer. O'Connor didn't let this hold her back. She worked hard as a lawyer and, later, a judge. In 1981, she was sworn in as the first female justice on the U.S. Supreme Court.

Almost 30 years later, the U.S. Supreme Court made history again when it welcomed its first Hispanic American justice. And this justice was also a woman. Sonia Sotomayor grew up in a working-class neighborhood and was taught to value education by her parents. After a successful career as a lawyer and judge, Sotomayor was nominated by President Barack Obama to become a Supreme Court justice because of her "extraordinary life."

AMAZING ACHIEVEMENTS

In 2009, Sotomayor became the first Hispanic American and third female justice on the Supreme Court.

Sonia Sotomayor

Sandra Day O'Connor

In 2015, the U.S. Supreme Court had three female justices: Ruth Bader Ginsberg, Elena Kagan, and Sonia Sotomayor.

CHEROKEE CHIEF

In 1985, Wilma Mankiller was the first woman to be elected principal chief of a major American Indian tribe. During the 10 years she served as principal chief of the Cherokee Nation, Mankiller helped double the tribe's membership.

Mankiller grew up poor in a home without electricity, plumbing, or telephones. Her family moved from land in Oklahoma to San Francisco, California, when she was young. There, she became involved in issues affecting Native Americans. She worked to raise money for prisoners and oversaw programs in local public schools.

In 1977, Mankiller moved back to Oklahoma and began working to improve the lives of her fellow Cherokees through health and education programs. As principal chief, Mankiller oversaw the tribe's large budget, which she invested back into government, education, and health care.

When Wilma Mankiller died in 2010, President Barack Obama remarked that she "served as an inspiration to women in Indian Country and across America."

AMAZING ACHIEVEMENTS

In 1998, President Bill Clinton awarded Wilma Mankiller the Presidential Medal of Freedom, which is the highest civilian honor in the United States.

A SCHOLAR'S PATH

Condoleezza Rice's first groundbreaking move came in 1993, when she became the first African American and first woman to serve as **provost** of Stanford University. Rice had grown up attending **segregated** schools in Birmingham, Alabama, but her passion for learning would eventually bring her to the top levels of government.

Rice earned a Ph.D., the highest-level college degree, in political science and became an expert on the Soviet Union. This led to her appointment to the National Security Council by President George H. W. Bush in 1989. In 2001, Bush's son, President George W. Bush, chose her as his national security advisor. In 2005, she became secretary of state. She was the first African American woman to serve in both positions.

AMAZING ACHIEVEMENTS

Rice was just 15 years old when she started college at the University of Denver. She originally intended to major in concert piano, but soon became interested in international politics.

Rice credits her parents with giving her high expectations in life despite the injustices of segregation. She once said, "My parents couldn't take me to have a hamburger at the Woolworth's lunch counter, but they had me absolutely convinced that I could be president…if I wanted to be."

FROM FIRST LADY TO SECRETARY OF STATE

Like Eleanor Roosevelt, Hillary Clinton originally became known in politics as a First Lady. She played an important role in her husband Bill Clinton's presidency from 1992 through 2000, but she had her own ambitions for the White House.

During her 12 years as the First Lady of Arkansas, while her husband was governor, Clinton worked as a lawyer while taking an active role in the state's politics. She became involved in national politics when Bill Clinton was elected president. In 1993, she chaired the Task Force on National Health Care Reform. Her health-care plan failed to gain approval from Congress, and some critics objected to her prominent position in her husband's presidency. Yet she continued to help create policy and traveled for U.S. international relations.

During her time as First Lady, Hillary Clinton played an important role in the passage of the State Children's Health Insurance Program and the Foster Care Independence Act. She also helped create the Office on Violence Against Women at the Department of Justice.

After her husband's presidency ended in 2000, Clinton became a U.S. senator for New York. This made her the first First Lady ever elected to the Senate, and she was reelected in 2006. She worked to gain better health benefits for veterans, bring Internet access to rural areas, and fund repairs and improvements to public schools.

In 2007, Clinton announced she was running for president. She was one of the leading Democratic candidates, but stepped down when Barack Obama gained the most support. After Obama won the presidential election and took office, he made Clinton his secretary of state. During her term, she visited more countries than any secretary of state before her and worked to improve women's and human rights around the world.

In April 2015, Clinton announced she was running for president once again. She has another chance to become the United States' first female president.

GAINING GROUND

Women have come a long way in American politics since Susan B. Anthony was arrested in 1872 for trying to vote. Though the United States hasn't yet elected a female president, women across the world are leading their country as head of state. German chancellor Angela Merkel is considered one of the most powerful people in the world, thanks to her central leadership role in the European Union.

As of 2015, there's still work to be done, however. Out of 100 U.S. senators, only 20 are women. Out of 435 members of the House of Representatives, only 84 are women. Women running for office still face more than their share of hurdles, but the chance to have a say in how your country is run is worth the fight.

Can you see yourself working in politics? One day, you may find yourself standing among these amazing women.

TIMELINE OF
WOMEN IN POLITICS

1848 - At the Seneca Falls Conference in New York, Elizabeth Cady Stanton demands women's right to vote.

1869 - Wyoming, not yet a state, becomes the first territory to grant women the right to vote. Utah follows in 1870.

1872 - Susan B. Anthony is arrested for illegally voting in a presidential election.

1916 - Jeanette Rankin becomes the first woman elected to the U.S. House of Representatives.

1920 - The United States ratifies the Nineteenth Amendment, guaranteeing the right to vote to all adult women.

1933 - Frances Perkins is appointed secretary of labor by President Franklin Delano Roosevelt, becoming the first female Cabinet member in the United States.

1960 - Sirimavo Bandaranaike is elected in Ceylon (now Sri Lanka), becoming the world's first female prime minister.

1968 - Shirley Chisholm becomes the first African American woman elected to Congress.

1972 - Chisholm becomes the first woman to seek the Democratic nomination for president.

1979 - Margaret Thatcher becomes the first female prime minister of Great Britain.

1985 - Wilma Mankiller becomes the first female principal chief of the Cherokee Nation.

1992 - Carol Moseley-Braun becomes the first African American woman elected to the Senate.

2000 - Hillary Clinton becomes the first First Lady elected to the Senate.

2006 - Nancy Pelosi becomes Speaker of the House, reaching a higher political rank than any other woman in U.S. history.

GLOSSARY

activist: A person who works to bring about change.

caucus: A group of people within the same political party that share the same concerns or interests.

civil rights: The rights of citizens to political and social freedom and equality.

disadvantaged: The state of being in unfortunate circumstances.

immigrant: A person who comes to live permanently in a different country.

minority: A relatively small group of people that belongs to a larger group.

pacifist: A person who does not support war or violence.

paralyze: To make unable to move.

primary: An election that chooses candidates to run for public office.

provost: A top official at a college or university.

relationship: The way in which two objects are connected.

segregated: Limited to members of one race.

slogan: A short, memorable phrase used in a political campaign.

Soviet Union: From 1922 to 1991, a country in eastern Europe and northern Asia that was a world superpower.

suffrage: The right to vote.

INDEX

WEBSITES

Due to the changing nature of Internet links, PowerKids Press has developed an online list of websites related to the subject of this book. This site is updated regularly. Please use this link to access the list: www.powerkidslinks.com/wmng/poli